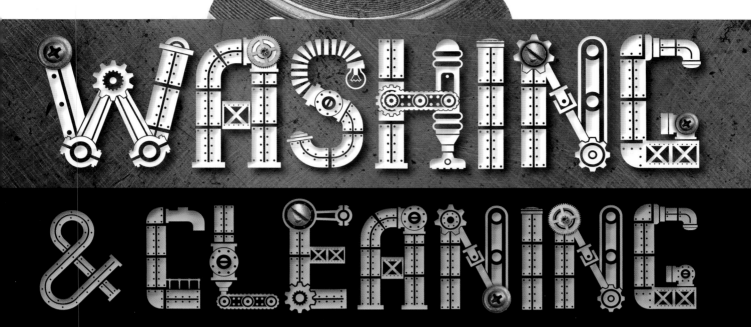

WASHING & CLEANING

BY ROBIN TWIDDY

BookLife
PUBLISHING

©2019
BookLife Publishing Ltd.
King's Lynn
Norfolk PE30 4LS
All rights reserved.
Printed in Malaysia.

A catalogue record for this
book is available from the
British Library.

ISBN: 9781-78637-625-1

Written by:
Robin Twiddy

Edited by:
Madeline Tyler

Designed by:
Gareth Liddington

CONTENTS

Words that look like this are explained in the glossary on page 31.

HOW CAN MACHINES CHANGE THE WORLD?

Today, it is easy to load our dishwashers and washing machines. We can even head out of the door to work or school and just forget about them. In fact, most people would say that washing machines, dishwashers and vacuum cleaners are the most boring things on the planet. Could the most boring things on the planet change the world for the better?

CREATE AND INNOVATE!

From simple machines to complex inventions, technology and machinery can solve problems, make life easier, and change <u>society</u>. Understanding the everyday machines we take for granted can help us understand the world around us a little better.

Why do we invent new things? We invent new machines to solve problems. Of course, when a new machine solves a big problem, it has the potential to change the world. Some of the machines that have changed the world are in your home — in your cupboards and in your kitchens.

Sometimes the technology used in one machine can lead to the creation of a completely different machine. Did you know that the technology used in radar machines in the Second World War led to the creation of the microwave oven? These inventions can lead to huge changes in society.

WASHING MACHINE FACT:

So many socks have gone missing in washing machines that scientists developed the 'Sock Loss Index' to figure out why socks go missing.

RADAR TO MICROWAVES!

THE SCIENCE OF WASHING

TO WET OR TO WASH?

The washing machine has had a surprisingly huge impact on society, but how does it work? There is more to washing clothes than just getting them wet. If that was all it took, our clothes would get clean every time we got caught out in the rain!

Maybe this isn't the most <u>efficient</u> way to do the laundry!

AGITATION IS THE KEY!

For clothes to become clean, the fibres need to be <u>agitated</u> to release the dirt. Heat also helps to loosen the dirt. So how do modern washing machines do this? You have probably noticed that your washing machine has a lot of settings – these control how fast the machine spins, the temperature of the water, how long the wash will last and more.

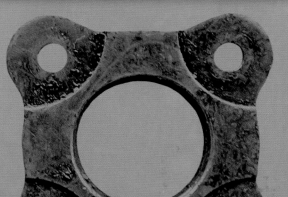

WHAT'S IN A WASHING MACHINE?

There are two drums in a washing machine. No, not musical drums. These are the kind that hold things.

Heating Element:
This heats the water to the programmed temperature.

Thermostat:
This <u>monitors</u> the temperature of the water.

Drum One:
This is the holey drum that spins to slosh the clothes around. It has holes in it to let the water in and out, and ridges that agitate the clothes.

Drum Two:
This is the outer drum. This drum contains the other drum. It doesn't spin and is watertight. The water feeds from this drum into the first drum.

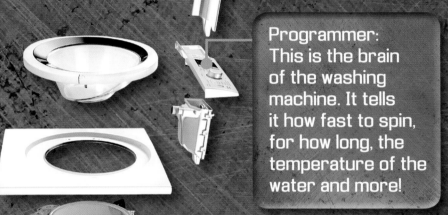

Programmer:
This is the brain of the washing machine. It tells it how fast to spin, for how long, the temperature of the water and more!

Electrically Operated Pump:
This pumps and drains the water in and out of the drum.

Motor:
This turns the first drum.

Pipes and Valves:
There is an in and out pipe. Each pipe has a valve inside it to control the flow of water.

WASHING THROUGH HISTORY

THE BEGINNING

The humble washing machine doesn't seem that exciting, does it? Well, it has a surprisingly interesting history. In ancient Mesopotamia, they used soap to wash their clothes as far back as 2800 B.C. Washing laundry was originally carried out in waterways, such as streams and rivers – this form of washing is still used today in <u>rural</u> areas.

This form of washing was very <u>labour intensive</u>. It took a lot of time and a lot of physical effort. Can you imagine how tiring doing the whole family's washing like this was? You might even be tempted to turn your pants inside out and get another week's wear out of them.

OPERATION MANUAL

- Carry clothes to the river by hand.
- Soak by hand.
- Apply soap by hand.
- Scrub clothes by hand.
- Beat wet clothes on hard surface by hand.
- Wring out by hand.
- Carry wet clothes back home by hand.

Do you help out with the washing in your house?

WHO DOES THE WASHING?

In many countries throughout the world, and throughout history, this kind of <u>domestic</u> task has been the responsibility of women. Washing the clothes of an entire household this way was very time consuming and left little time for anything else. After people first started washing their clothes, it was thousands of years before the first labour-saving machine was invented.

THE WASHBOARD

The first known use of a washboard was in Scandinavia in the 1800s. The washboard was a board – made from either wood or metal – with ridges that wet clothes could be scrubbed over. The washboard meant that the scrubbing and agitation needed to clean clothes could easily be done at home.

Even with the washboard, doing the laundry could still take all day!

OPERATION MANUAL

- Gather water from the well or river by hand.
- Boil water.
- Soak by hand.
- Apply soap by hand.
- Scrub using washboard.
- Wring out water by hand.

SAVING TIME ON DRYING

So, the introduction of the washboard saved some time, but wringing out wet clothes was still a tough and time-consuming job. Some types of clothes press already existed. These would squeeze the water out of clothes, but they often required more than one person to use them.

Wringing out clothes by hand must have been quite a workout!

Mangles could be dangerous if you caught your hair or a finger in the rollers... Ouch!

THE HAND MANGLE

The mechanical mangle became available to the most people in the early 19th century. The user would turn a hand crank that would turn gears, moving two large rollers. The wet clothes would be fed between the rollers, squeezing the water out and flattening the clothes at the same time.

OPERATION MANUAL

- Gather water from the well or river by hand.
- Boil water.
- Soak by hand.
- Apply soap by hand.
- Scrub using washboard.
- Ring out water using hand-cranked mangle.

THE MANUAL
WASHING MACHINE

1851 saw the invention of the very first washing machine, but it was very different to the washing machines that we are familiar with. This washing machine was hand-powered, like the mangle. It had a drum that was filled with water and rotated. It also had paddles that could agitate the clothes.

SMALL IMPROVEMENTS

This new washing machine meant that people could wash larger loads than they could with the washboard. Each new invention would make this process a little bit easier each time. However, the washing machine would soon see a big change.

OPERATION MANUAL

- Gather water from the well or river by hand.
- Boil water.
- Soak in washing machine.
- Apply soap to washing machine.
- Agitate in washing machine with hand crank.
- Ring out water using hand-cranked mangle.

THE ELECTRIC WASHING MACHINE

By the late 1800s, thanks to Thomas Edison, more and more homes in the US had access to electricity. Because of this, the first <u>commercial</u> electric washing machine was released in 1907. Its name? Thor!

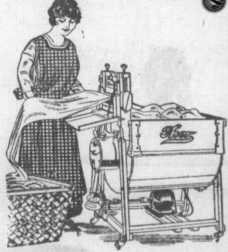

The Thor

Electric Washing and Wringing Machine

Does the entire family washing at a saving of money,

This is a 1917 advertisement for the Thor electric washing machine.

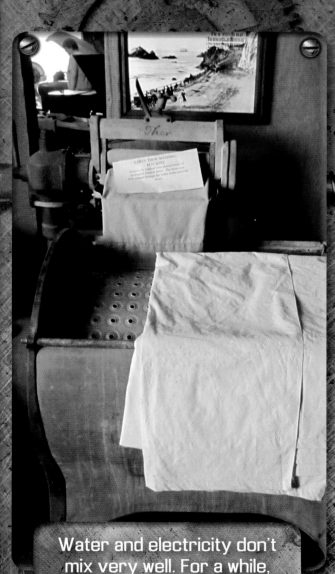

Water and electricity don't mix very well. For a while, people were risking their lives just to do the washing!

THOR, THE GOD OF...WASHING?

Thor had an electric motor that turned the drum. Although this was a huge leap forward, the user still needed to add soap by hand and use a hand-powered mangle. The early models didn't have a waterproof motor and would often <u>short-circuit</u>, which could be very dangerous.

WASHING MACHINE FACT:

Astronauts burn their underwear! Because there are no washing machines in space, astronauts put their dirty clothes in the rubbish, which burns up on re-entry to Earth's atmosphere.

FASTER, FASTER

By 1920, the electric washing machine had become safer and a faster spin was added. This faster spin used centrifugal force to draw a lot of the water out of the clothes. But what is centrifugal force? How do you feel when you go around a roundabout in a car? Your body wants to keep going outwards doesn't it? This is because of inertia. Inertia is the force that makes an object want to keep travelling in the same direction rather than turning. It is this force that pulls the water out through the holes in the drum wall of a washing machine.

The chairs on this ride are pulled out and up by the centrifugal force.

MOTORISED MANGLE

Around the same time, an electric motor was added to the mangle. This made it much easier to operate. People had to be even more careful with the electric mangle. You really don't want to catch your hair in there!

OPERATION MANUAL

- Place clothes into drum.
- Apply soap to washing machine.
- Soak in washing machine.
- Switch on washing machine.
- Empty soapy water.
- Add clean water and rinse.
- Ring out water using electric mangle.

13

REFINING THE WASHING MACHINE

By the 1940s, 60 percent of houses in the United States had an electric washing machine. Although these machines made the laundry process a lot easier, they still required constant attention to make sure that they didn't overflow or jam. People also still had to empty the soap and add clean water by hand.

Can you imagine having to regularly check if the washing machine was flooding the kitchen or had become stuck again?

AUTOMATION

However, the 1950s brought a new feature to the machine: automation. Automatic washing machines can carry out all the washing tasks without needing human help. A program starts the machine, a pressure switch makes sure that the machine isn't overloaded by water, a thermostat <u>regulates</u> the water temperature and a timer controls when the machine starts and stops.

WASHING AND DRYING... WOW, WHAT A NOVELTY!

Since the 1950s, washing machines have been made to be more and more efficient by using less water and electricity. However, only the wealthiest homes could afford these wonders of washing until the prices dropped ten years later. It wasn't long until a dryer function was added, and the machine could then wash and dry all in one.

That's a lot less work than a trip to the river!

THERE'S MORE TO CHANGING THE WORLD THAN BETTER TECHNOLOGY

Although these <u>innovations</u> were amazing in themselves, the most important way that the washing machine changed the world was not technologically. New washing machines also had many <u>social</u> impacts that changed the world in some amazing ways. The effects of the washing machine would soon be seen throughout society.

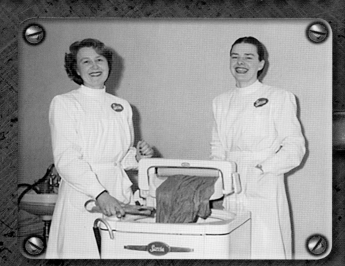

OPERATION MANUAL

- Place clothes into machine.
- Set program and timer.
- Add soap to washing machine.
- Walk away.

TO WASH OR WORK?

For a long time, domestic chores in many places around the world were the responsibility of women. Running a house was a full-time job and many women wouldn't have been able to find the time to work as well. If they did work, it would often be cooking and cleaning in the homes of richer people.

WORKING WOMEN

When the First World War began, lots of <u>working-class</u> men in England were called into service. This means that they had to join the army or navy. Because of this, factories, offices and other workplaces were understaffed. This led to more women than ever starting work to replace the men that had gone to war.

This continued throughout the Second World War, when more and more women got jobs and started work.

DO IT OURSELVES?

As many working-class women were needed in understaffed workplaces, the women of richer households suddenly found themselves without servants and maids to do their washing and cleaning. This meant that they needed to learn to manage their own homes. At this point, only richer families could afford things like washing machines.

For many wealthy women, having to do the chores came as a shock.

FINALLY AFFORDABLE

As more and more families bought washing machines and other labour-saving products, prices began to go down and these machines became more affordable. By the 1950s, many more people could afford newer and better washing machines, freeing many women up to be able to go to work full-time.

VACUUM CLEANERS: DO THEY SUCK?

MORE TO THE VACUUM CLEANER THAN YOU THOUGHT

These loud, pet-frightening machines have changed the way that people keep their houses clean. The technology used in making these cleaning machines is now used all over the world and even up in space to help astronauts take care of some important business.

Jump to page 27 if you want to find out what vacuum cleaner technology helps astronauts do.

WHY DID WE NEED THE VACUUM CLEANER?

The vacuum cleaner was a solution to a problem that appeared in the late 1700s, when carpets became popular. Before this, the good old-fashioned broom was enough to take care of the job of cleaning the average home. But carpets created a new problem. If you can't clean it with a broom, then how do you clean it?

Carpets helped hide any dust for a while and didn't need to be cleaned as often as floors needed to be swept.

THE SCIENCE OF SUCKING!

So, what is going on inside this dust-busting device?

Most vacuum cleaners are powered from the mains power supply. When it is switched on, an electric motor inside powers a fan.

The fan causes suction inside the body of the vacuum cleaner — sucking air through the hose. Dirt is pulled up and through the vacuum cleaner by this suction.

Some vacuum cleaners have a rotating brush that is driven by a rubber belt attached to the motor. This rotating brush beats dirt out of the carpet and up into the air flow.

The air flows through the bag and out through vents in the body. The bag acts like a filter catching the dirt.

Although vacuum cleaners come in all shapes and sizes, almost all of them are based on this same design and these basic <u>principles</u>. So how did we go from the old-fashioned broom to the modern vacuum cleaner?

A woman from Kent in the UK used the same vacuum cleaner for over 70 years!

BEFORE THE VACUUM CLEANER

THE CARPET SWEEPER

The first carpet sweeper was invented in 1860 by Daniel Hess. It was just a rotating brush and <u>bellows</u>. This was the first step towards the vacuum cleaner that we all know today. It used rotating brushes and a <u>vacuum</u> created by a bellows system to suck dust up then blow it into a trap.

Bellows create a vacuum when they are expanded. Air is then pulled in to fill the space.

CARPET BEATING

Before the invention of the carpet sweeper, and eventually the vacuum cleaner, people had to take their rugs and carpets outside to clean them by beating them with a carpet beater. Can you imagine dragging all your rugs and carpets outside, hanging them up and beating them with something that looked like a small tennis racket?

ROLL UP, ROLL UP
– GET YOUR CARPETS CLEANED

Just like washing clothes by hand, cleaning carpets by hand was physically hard and time consuming. It wasn't long before someone created a machine to make the job easier. In 1898, John S. Thurman invented a gasoline-powered carpet cleaner. There was only one problem with it — the size!

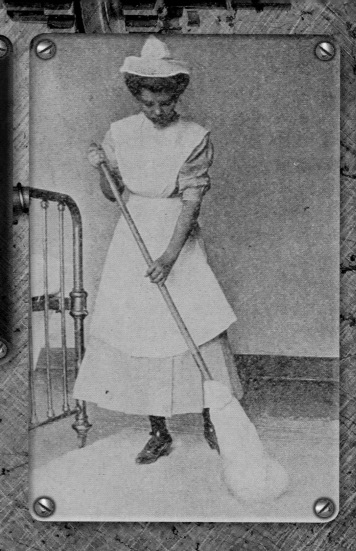

THIS VACUUM BLOWS

This gasoline-powered cleaner was so big that it needed to be pulled by a horse and cart. Unlike the cleaners that followed it, Thurman's worked by blowing instead of sucking. Another inventor, Hubert Cecil Booth, asked Thurman why his cleaner blew the dust instead of sucking it up. Apparently, Thurman became quite upset and said that "sucking out dust was impossible" and that it had "been tried over and over again without success" before storming off!

THE PUFFING BILLY

Three years later, in 1901, Booth released his 'Puffing Billy', which became the first vacuum cleaner to prove Thurman wrong. His vacuum cleaner was also huge like Thurman's and needed a horse and cart to pull it around. For a price, the Puffing Billy could be hired. It would be parked in the street outside the business or home and a team of workers would feed sucking tubes through the windows.

PROVING
THURMAN WRONG

The Puffing Billy used an <u>internal combustion engine</u>. This powered a piston pump that pulled the air through a piece of cloth that caught the dust. This was a huge breakthrough and meant the Puffing Billy was in direct competition with Thurman. Booth's innovation and basic design for using a vacuum is the basis for all vacuum cleaners that followed.

THE DOMESTIC CYCLE

The next big innovation to the vacuum cleaner came from Walter Griffiths in 1905. He made a vacuum cleaner that could be carried by hand — making it much more <u>convenient</u> for home owners. The innovations didn't stop there — only a year later, the 'Domestic Cyclone' was released. This used water to catch the dirt, making sure that it didn't escape into the air.

This is an early compact vacuum cleaner by Electric Suction Sweeper Company, from around 1908.

REINVENTED

The real breakthrough in vacuum cleaning came from James Spangler, a cleaner from Canton, Ohio, in the US. Spangler's design improved on existing designs to make the vacuum cleaner much more effective and easier to use. His electric rotating brush kicked the dirt up from the carpet to be sucked in by the vacuum.

THE RISE OF HOOVER

A VACUUM BY ANY OTHER NAME

Spangler couldn't afford to make the machine himself, so he sold the design to William Henry Hoover. Hoover made a few minor redesigns and then made a fortune from the invention. Eventually, Hoover's product was so popular that people started referring to the vacuum cleaner simply as a 'hoover'!

MAKING DUST DISAPPEAR

The innovations didn't stop there. While the vacuum cleaner made keeping a dust-free home a much easier and less demanding task, future innovations made it even easier. Miniature vacuum cleaners make taking care of small messes easy, while robotic vacuum cleaners have done away with physically vacuuming completely.

Robot Vacuum Cleaner

ALWAYS IMPROVING

Since Hoover purchased the design from Spangler in 1908, the vacuum cleaner has been reinvented over and over again; it's been made smaller, lighter and quieter. Whether you call it a vac, vacuum cleaner or sucking machine, nearly everyone has one in their homes now.

VACUUM CLEANERS
PROTECTING OUR HOMES

So, how did the vacuum cleaner change the world? Like the washing machine, it helped to make some long and difficult chores in the home quicker and easier. They also helped to make the home more <u>hygienic</u>. Carpets gather lots of dust, <u>bacteria</u> and other things that can cause illnesses and allergies. This really benefitted people with asthma and allergies.

THE MODERN VACUUM CLEANER!

DIFFERENT VACUUM CLEANERS FOR DIFFERENT JOBS

Now there are many types of vacuum cleaner available.

Canister vacuums are used for small areas of carpet and hard floors.

Steam vacuum cleaners use steam and hot water to clean carpets whilst removing dirt.

Robotic vacuums use sensors to <u>navigate</u> homes and clean automatically.

Handheld vacuums are cordless and perfect for small, on-the-go cleaning jobs, such as spills.

Pet vacuum cleaners are made to lift thick pet hair from carpets.

MORE TO THE VACUUM THAN MEETS THE EYE

Don't think that the use of the vacuum ends with cleaning. Oh no — some very clever people have found some surprising and exciting ways to use this technology in other places. For instance: the space toilet! Space toilets use vacuum technology to stop... things... floating away!

BUILDING
WITH VACUUMS

How did the humble vacuum cleaner revolutionise <u>manufacturing</u>? By adding a suction cup to the vacuum, almost any material can then be lifted, moved, rotated and handled in almost any way you can imagine. Vacuums are used on lots of production lines, making all sorts of different things.

HONOURABLE MENTIONS

SUPER CLEANERS

There are so many machines that have changed our lives, and the world, for the better. Here are a few more.

The pressurised hose shoots out pressurised water. It uses an electric pump that pulls water from the tap and then pushes it out of the hose at a high speed. It then blasts the dirt off the surface that is being cleaned!

Pressure Hose

Floor Buffer

The floor buffer creates clean, shiny surfaces on hard floors. It works in a surprisingly simple way. Floors that are covered in a thin layer of polymer (a hard plastic coating) get dents and dings from wear and tear. This makes the surface dull. The floor buffer uses <u>abrasive</u> pads that are spun at high speeds by an electric motor to strip away a thin layer, leaving a smooth surface.

The air scrubber is a machine which filters the air, removing harmful gases, mould and pollution. It sucks in air, traps the nasty particles, and blows the clean air back into the room.

As the air outside becomes dirtier, we may all need an air scrubber in our homes.

A professional car wash can clean your car in a fraction of the time it would take you by hand. By using a combination of water sprayers and automatic scrubbers, car washes have made cleaning your car an easy job. It's also really fun to sit inside the car whilst the machines go to work!

COULD YOU LIVE IN A WORLD WITHOUT MACHINES?

A WORLD WITHOUT WASHING MACHINES

Could you do the laundry without the help of our machine friends?

To give it a try, you will need:
- A large bucket
- Some dirty clothes
- Either a hard, clean surface or a washboard
- Some detergent or soap

Make sure that you have a an adult to help you as this can be quite hard and messy. You might find that it is harder than you think.

A WORLD WITHOUT VACUUM CLEANERS

Do you think you are strong enough to clean a carpet in the traditional way?

To give it a try, you will need:
- A dusty rug
- Something to use as a rug beater (an old tennis racket will do the job)
- Somewhere to hang your rug (a climbing frame or hand rail will do)
- A mask to wear on your face if your rug is extra dusty!

GLOSSARY

abrasive	rough and textured surface used to wear away or polish a surface
agitated	to cause something to move fast through force, such as to shake something
bacteria	microscopic living things that can cause diseases
bellows	a bag that can be expanded to pull air in and squeezed to push air out
commercial	having to do with trade, business and making money
convenient	easily used and fulfils a need without much effort
domestic	to do with the home
efficient	getting the most out of something in the best way possible
hygienic	clean and free of bacteria that is harmful to health
innovations	things that have not been done before
internal combustion engine	an engine in which fuel is burned to release energy
labour intensive	something that takes a lot of physical energy and time
manufacturing	making large quantities of something
monitors	to watch, check, or keep track of something
navigate	travel around with knowledge of your surroundings
principles	a set of rules that shape behaviour
regulates	controls and maintains
rural	relating to or characteristic of the countryside
short-circuit	the failure of electricity to flow properly because the wires or connections in the circuit are damaged
social	relating to a group of people or a community
society	a collection of people living together at a certain time
vacuum	a space empty of matter
working-class	a class of people that make up the main workforce in a society

INDEX